We've got a really big show. Nip it in the bud. God will get you for that. Oh, my nose! The truth is out there. Danger Will Robinson! Sit on it. Elizabeth, I'm coming to join ya! Kiss my grits! What you see is what you get. You rang? Let's be careful out there. Up your nose with a rubber hose. Who loves ya, baby? How you doin'? Is that your final answer? You look mahvelous. Sock it to me. Norm! The thrill of victory, the agony of defeat. Smile, you're on *Candid Camera*. De plane! De plane! Come on down! Yada, yada, yada!

TV Land LEGENDS

Book 'em, Danno! Dynomite! Ayyy! Yabba Dabba Do! What you talking 'bout, Willis? Heeere's Johnny! What's happenin'!! You bet your bippy. Live from New York...Lucy, you have some 'splainin' to do. Well, isn't that special?! Zoicks! They killed Kenny! One of these days, Alice, Pow! Right in the kisser. You're fired! D'oh! It's a beautiful day in the neighborhood. Champagne wishes and caviar dreams! Cowabunga! Cut, it, out. Did I do that? Eat my shorts. Yowza, yowza, yowza. Heyyy Yooou Guuys!!! Homey don't play that. Nanoo Nanoo Sorry about that, Chief. Beam me up, Scotty. And that's the way it is. Say Goodnight, Gracie. Baby, you're the greatest! No soup for you! Good night and good luck. Gee, Mrs. Cleaver. Pork chops and apple sauce. Space, the final frontier...to boldly go where no man has gone before. Good night, John Boy. We've got a really big show. Nip it in the bud. God will get you for that. Oh, my nose! The truth is out there. Danger Will Robinson! Sit on it. Elizabeth, I'm coming to join ya! Kiss my grits! Up your nose with a rubber hose.

TVLand LEGENDS

New York   London   Toronto   Sydney

Bill Cosby, photographed by Eddie Adams, 2003

POCKET BOOKS, a division of Simon & Schuster, Inc.
1230 Avenue of the Americas, New York, NY 10020

Produced by Melcher Media, Inc.

Copyright © 2006 by Viacom International Inc.

All rights reserved, including the right to reproduce
this book or portions thereof in any form whatsoever.
For information address Pocket Books, 1230 Avenue
of the Americas, New York, NY 10020

Library of Congress Control Number: 2006904352

ISBN-13: 978-1-4165-3153-1
ISBN-10: 1-4165-3153-X

First Pocket Books hardcover edition November 2006

10 9 8 7 6 5 4 3 2 1

POCKET and colophon are registered trademarks of
Simon & Schuster, Inc.

Printed in China

For information regarding special discounts for bulk purchases, please contact
Simon & Schuster Special Sales at 1-800-456-6798 or business@simonandschuster.com

the icons contents

candice bergen
fred rogers
jim henson
robin williams
carl reiner
bob hope
eddie murphy
roseanne barr
barbara eden and larry hagman
jack benny and marilyn monroe
ed sullivan
diahann carroll
henry winkler
david janssen
rod serling
leonard nimoy
william shatner
ron howard
don knotts and andy griffith
joan collins
farrah fawcett
on bill cosby by touré
bill cosby

 icons

phylicia rashad
sarah jessica parker
goldie hawn
flip wilson
the moms
richard pryor
mary tyler moore
elizabeth montgomery
alfred hitchcock
peter falk
ted koppel
mike wallace
james garner
michael landon
art carney
ray romano
michael j. fox
jean stapleton and carroll o'connor
desmond wilson and redd foxx
bob newhart
george burns and gracie allen

the programs

cheers
leave it to beaver
the brady bunch
everybody loves raymond
roots
dallas
desperate housewives
frasier
the sopranos
laverne and shirley
friends
the westerns
hogan's heroes
gunsmoke
the muppet show
the odd couple
will and grace
the sonny and cher show

the jeffersons
the addams family
the munsters
group therapy by mary tyler moore
the mary tyler moore show
the avengers
get smart
mission impossible
nypd blue
the mod squad
the tv cops/detectives
saturday night live
in living color
monty python's flying circus
rowan & martin's laugh-in

foreword by larry jones, president of TV Land

When you are a newborn, your eyes can only focus well on objects about twelve inches away. That happens to be just the distance from a nursing baby to its mother's face. Studying a face, with all its nuances and meanings, is our first, vital learning. Of course, before you know it, your ability to focus improves and Mom is telling you not to sit so close to the set.

The TV set. Now new faces come before us fast and furious. Sure, there are faces in our daily lives—but the ones on TV are more fun. Smiling, frowning, laughing, winking. Our studies continue; we learn new faces, new subtleties. Faces that reveal the first inkling of a sure-fire scheme, or the slowly dawning realization that this is the boss's wife. The coy sidelong glance of potential romance. The unflinching stare of a fearless lawman. The deadpan take that so delightfully masks internal chaos.

We learn to read every little cue, anticipate every shift in motivation. We learn to empathize with the downtrodden and to distrust the smarmy, slick, and ingratiating. We learn to laugh at the hopelessly naïve, the thoroughly obtuse, the pompous who are headed for a fall, the blusterers, the fast-talkers, the fish out of water, the loveable whiners, and that one level-headed fellow surrounded by a maddening group of eccentrics.

All those faces on our televisions. Thousands of faces. Some were passing acquaintances, familiar but inconsequential. But with some we forged relationships. True and deep relationships. With each of these, the face was imprinted onto our consciousness forever, indelible, unforgettable, and unchangeable.

And these are the TV Land Legends.

Look into those impossibly familiar faces. Lucille Ball. Bill Cosby. Carol Burnett. Walter Cronkite. Roseanne. Sally Field. Eddie Murphy. Art Carney. Mister Rogers. In a glance, you are carried to their world, brought inside their unique perspective, told a piece of their personal truth.

Each of these photographs tells a story. In many ways, they cut deeper to the bone than any moving, dancing, fluid television image ever could. Lucy hiding behind the mask of "The Little Tramp" who came before her. Sarah Jessica Parker playing dress-up ballerina like a little girl. Don Adams pretending he is taller than Barbara Feldon—who lets him. The early cast of *Saturday Night Live* taunting us with their not-ready-for-prime-time, too-cool-to-mug-for-the-cameras attitude.

Some of these photographs simply capture the essence of the characters: Wally and the Beaver in all their gleaming, well-scrubbed purity. Others capture the actors at play: the nonstop clowning of Milton Berle at the height of his charisma and 50 years later and 180 degrees away, the detached self-mocking irony of Conan O'Brien as a shirt model. Still other photos take us behind the cameras, away from familiar TV settings to capture rarities: Johnny Carson at his drums, the dour Alfred Hitchcock cracking a rare smile.

This collection is not an argument. There are a hundred more faces who have every right to be included, and every day there is the possibility that a new star has emerged from the inky shadows to join the constellation. *TV Land* Legends is, in itself, a snapshot, a moment in time that compresses 50 years of television into a hundred or so photographs.

So grab the best seat, adjust your vertical hold, and stay tuned because coming right up is *TV Land Legends*.

the icons

danny
devito **on** danny devito

"I read the [*Taxi*] script and I thought, This was a magnificent—this is a fun character of Louie, this guy. So they said, 'You're going to go in and meet these guys,' and I didn't know what to expect. They were in this well-appointed office; it was just beautiful. I saw the hot seat over there where the actor is going to go sit and read his lines for the producers. So I walked in the room and I said, 'One thing I want to know before we start: Who wrote this shit?' and I threw it on the table. I got the job. I didn't have to work for it."

Danny DeVito, photographed by George Lange, 1997

Milton Berle, circa 1950

Oprah Winfrey, photographed by Cliff Watts, 2005

billy crystal

a tribute to sid caesar

The first time I saw Sid was on *Your Show of Shows* in the early fifties. *The King and I* was the hot movie at the time, and Yul Brynner its hot star. So of course Sid did a takeoff on *The King and I*, and there was this palace set, and Sid made his entrance as Yul. Bald wig, the capri pants, and bare feet. He struck the king's pose and then suddenly grabbed his bare foot and started screaming, 'Who's smoking in the palace?' It was hilarious; I was hooked. Even though I was young, I wanted to do what Sid did, and his cast of Carl Reiner and Howard Morris and Imogene Coca; I wanted to be funny like Sid was funny.

He could do anything, be anybody. From the German professor to Progress Hornsby, a very stoned jazz musician who had someone in his group on radar to warn them in case they approached the melody. He could talk in any language, it seemed, play any kind of character. It was a great time for funny people on TV. My folks let us stay up late on school nights to watch Sid and the other giants, but it was Sid who to me was the greatest, a comedy force of nature.

His energy, his commitment to being dangerous and yet so real, was breathtaking. He was like my crazy relatives, except he would buy retail. So many years later, the brilliance of Sid and his genius sidekicks, and the writing of Mel Brooks and Neil Simon and Larry Gelbart and Woody Allen, among others on that staff, is still as funny today as it was back then. He is timeless.

He is my hero. I was lucky; I grew up in a time when Caesar ruled the vast empire called television. You usually see your heroes from afar—you rarely get to know them. I can't tell you how much it means to me, as that little kid watching Sid Caesar so many years ago, on that black and white screen, that I have the honor of knowing him, and now to publicly thank him. And my parents for letting me stay up late to watch him. I'm not sure what kind of comedy I would have done if I had not seen Sid Caesar. I don't know if I would be a comic at all. Funny is a precious metal, and Sid has always been and will always remain the gold standard.

Sid Caesar and Imogene Coca, photographed by Firooz Zahedi, 1995

Lucille Ball, 1962

Ellen DeGeneres, photographed by Nigel Parry, 2001

Will Smith, photographed by Annie Leibovitz, 1999

Larry David, photographed by Jill Greenberg, 2005

Jimmie Walker, 1975

paul mooney ON▶ jimmie walker

"Blacks finally had something they could call their own with that show. You had a major star in Jimmie Walker on the show. *Good Times* was in an era of great creativity. It was a brilliant time."

Freddie Prinze, 1974

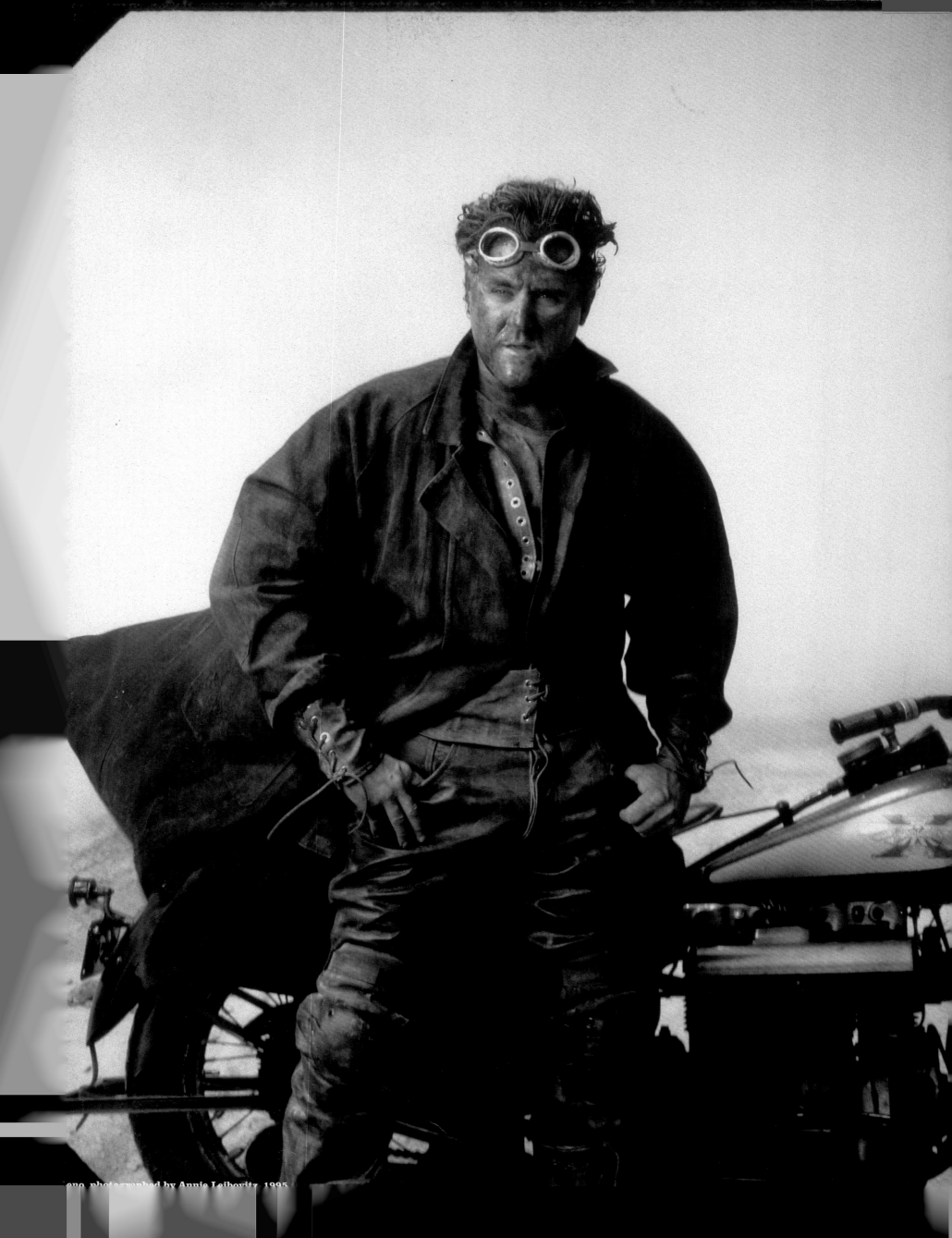

 jack paar

"I asked Jack once, 'What's the formula for how to handle things when you don't like a guest?' He said: 'You think of it as what you would do in real life. Smile, be nice, and then suddenly kick 'em under the table.'"

Jack Paar, photographed by Nigel Parry, 1997

Ed Asner, *circa* 1980

Tom Brokaw, Dan Rather, and Peter Jennings, photographed by Annie Leibovitz, 1995

Dick Van Dyke and Mary Tyler Moore, photographed by Annie Leibovitz, 1995

Carol Burnett, photographed by Jack Chuck, 1995

 **megan mullally on → carol burnett**

"As a kid growing up in Oklahoma City, the great *Carol Burnett Show* was on Monday nights at nine central time. However, my bedtime was also nine central time. So, because it was my favorite show, my mom would put me to bed at eight and I'd sleep for an hour, then she would wake me back up at nine so I could watch. And I feel like the fact that I was exposed to great talent like Carol Burnett has helped make me who I am. Whatever I've been lucky enough to achieve started there, in front of the television set in Oklahoma City."

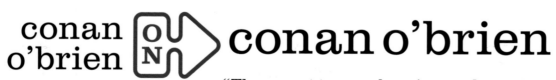

conan o'brien

"The secret to our show is people are two-thirds asleep, and they're seeing it, and they're not sure if they really saw what really happened."

Conan O'Brien, photographed by Gavin Bond, 2005

Larry King, courtesy of Michael O'Neill for *Vanity Fair*, 1995

Dick Clark, photographed by Paul Schutzer, 1958

Edward R. Murrow, 1955

david letterman ON ▷ johnny carson

"*The Tonight Show* didn't become *The Tonight Show* until Johnny did it. He created the template for that show, and everybody else who is doing a show, myself included, we're all kind of secretly doing Johnny's *Tonight Show*. And the reason we're all doing Johnny's *Tonight Show* is because you think, Well, if I do Johnny's *Tonight Show*, maybe I'll be a little like Johnny and people will like me more. But it sadly doesn't work that way. If you're not Johnny, you're wasting your time."

Johnny Carson, 1956

Howard Cosell and Muhammad Ali, 1970

Phil Donahue, date unknown

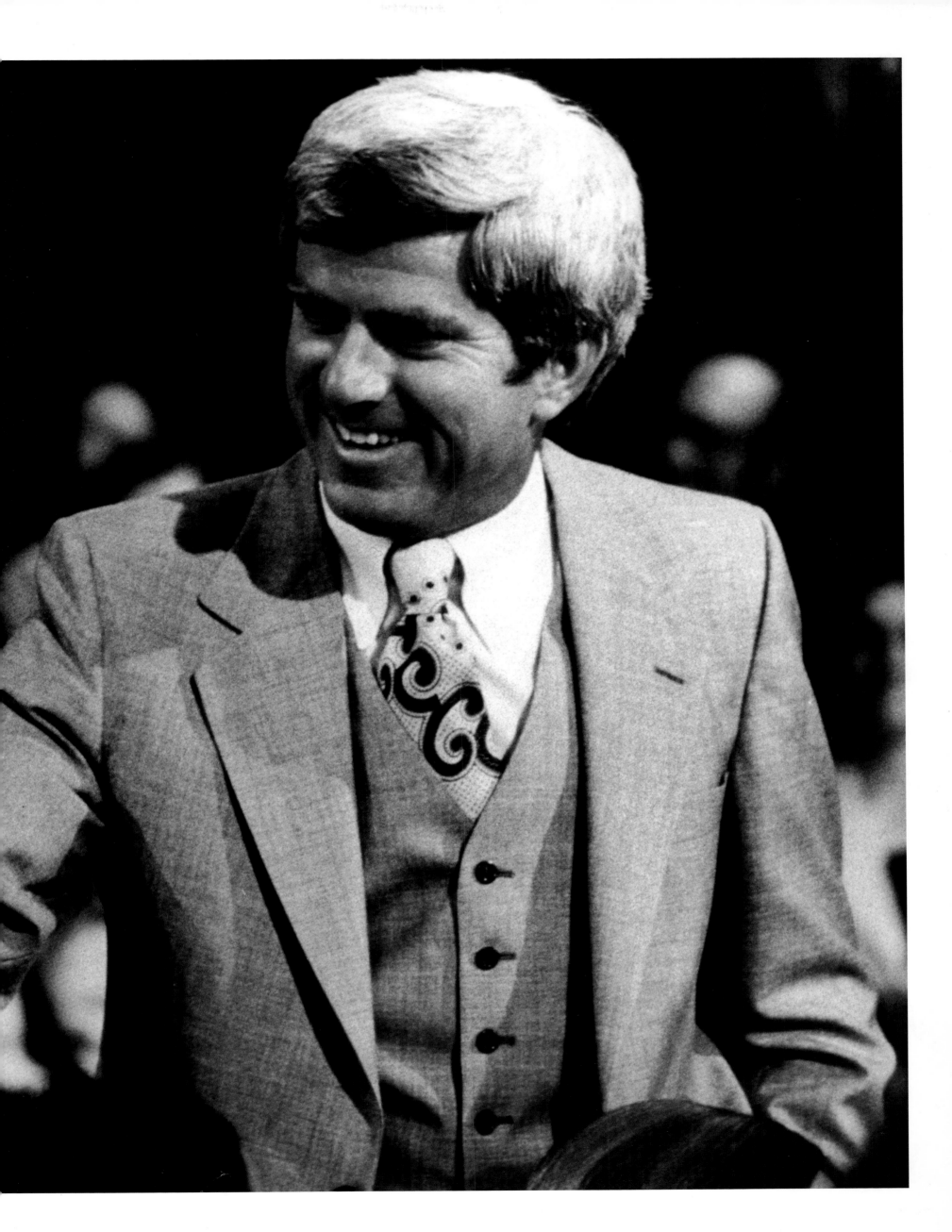

Alan Alda, as *M*A*S*H*'s Hawkeye, photographed by Gene Trindl, 1974

alan alda

"Even after days of rehearsal [for *M*A*S*H*], I was still wondering: How am I supposed to be this guy who seems totally unlike me? He drinks, he chases women, he's a smart aleck. And what's he thinking, what does he want? I had to get out of this damn shed. Look, I thought, how different am I from him? We're all human, right? We all have the same impulses. . . ."

Raymond Burr, photographed by Yousuf Karsh, 1960

Bea Arthur, 1974

Walter Cronkite, courtesy of Michael O'Neill for *Vanity Fair*, 1995

Katie Couric, photographed by Jonathan Skow, 2002

Barbara Walters, photographed by Yousuf Karsh, 1972

Andy Rooney, photographed by Platon, 2003

Bob Denver, as *Gilligan's Island's* Gilligan, 1965

Sally Field, as *The Flying Nun's* Sister Bertrille, 1968

Candice Bergen and Charlie McCarthy, photographed by Mary Ellen Mark, 1978

Fred Rogers and King Friday, 1960

Jim Henson and Kermit the Frog, 1978

Robin Williams, photographed by Firooz Zahedi, 1993

Carl Reiner, 1955

dick
van dyke

(on)

bob hope

"Bob Hope, like Mark Twain, had a sense of humor that was uniquely American, and like Twain, we'll likely never see another like him."

Bob Hope, photographed by Annie Leibovitz, 1995

Eddie Murphy, photographed by Timothy White, 1996

dave
chappelle **ON** eddie murphy

"Another guy that works real hard will get a sitcom or he'll get
a shot, just by merit of showing up and by putting the work in.
He'll get a shot. But he'll never be like Eddie Murphy."

Roseanne Barr, photographed by Peggy Sirota, 2001

Barbara Eden and Larry Hagman,
as *I Dream of Jeannie's* Captain Tony
Nelson and Jeannie, 1965

Jack Benny and Marilyn Monroe, 1954

joseph cates ON⊳ ed sullivan

producer

"Ed Sullivan was the Zeigfeld of our era. He didn't have a personality, but he didn't need one. He got the acts, and to get the acts you have to understand the country and the times. He did, and he was better at it than anybody else."

Ed Sullivan with dancer, photographed by Allan Grant, 1958

Diahann Carroll, 1960

Henry Winkler, photographed by John R. Hamilton, 1974

The license plate reads: CALIFORNIA YND 085

David Janssen, photographed by Gene Trindl, 1965

Rod Serling, 1960

Leonard Nimoy, photographed by Lillian Elaine Wilson, 2003

William Shatner, photographed by Jeffery Newbury, 1994

Ron Howard, photographed by Xavier Torres-Bacchetta, 2005

Don Knotts and Andy Griffith, 1965

Joan Collins, 1960

Farrah Fawcett, photographed by Henry Groskinsky, 1978

touré ON▷ bill cosby

No one in the history of television has had more shows with their name in the title than Bill Cosby. Besides *The Cosby Show*, that mammoth NBC comedy starring the upper-middle-class Huxtable family, there was *The Bill Cosby Show*, *The New Bill Cosby Show*, *The Cosby Mysteries*, *Fat Albert and the Cosby Kids*, *Cosby*, and *Cos*. But after eight shows with his name on them Bill Cosby is still not seen as a Trumpesque egomaniac. He's a modern Walt Disney. When you see the Cosby name, it's a promise of wholesome family entertainment—you know nothing offensive will follow.

America's Favorite Dad was a standup comic in the '60s, telling stories about his childhood in the ghetto of North Philly without using dirty language or invoking racially charged sentiments. He told universal stories and, like Sidney Poitier, he was nonthreatening, but still cool, and all that allowed Cosby to break barriers. In 1965 he debuted as undercover CIA Agent Alexander Scott on NBC's *I Spy*, alongside Robert Culp's undercover Agent Kelly Robinson. Cosby won three consecutive Emmys for Outstanding Lead in a Dramatic Series, proving his acting chops. Though *I Spy* made Cosby the first black actor to star in a dramatic series, his race was never an issue and his character wasn't subservient to Culp's. That's always been the Cosby way onscreen: present the flavor of blackness without the implicit challenge to white authority as seen in the onstage persona of others like Richard Pryor. But Cosby never seems to struggle with whether or not he's equal to whites—he knows he is—and thus, while his characters are easygoing, he never allows them to be docile or deferential.

One of Cosby's comedy routines from the '60s was about a childhood friend from Philly whom he called Fat Albert. In 1972 Cosby brought the character to life in *Fat Albert and the Cosby Kids*, an animated show that ran on Saturday mornings on CBS. It featured Cosby as the live-action host and the voice of several characters, including Fat Albert, Mushmouth, and Mudfoot. Fat Albert and his friends, the Junkyard Gang, lived in the 'hood and had to deal with con artists, drug use, and gun violence, during a much more halcyon time.

Through the '70s and early '80s, as Cosby's four daughters and one son grew up, he learned the joys and pains of being a parent. In 1984 he brought those stories to the small screen with *The Cosby Show*, featuring the Huxtables, a family that mirrored his own, with four daughters and one son. As TV lore has it, Cosby planned on the Huxtable patriarch being a janitor or a chauffeur until his wife, Camille, told him to play a doctor, thus opening the door to TV's first well-educated, well-paid, unabashedly intellectual black family. Dr. Cliff Huxtable was an OB/GYN who lived in a million-dollar Brooklyn townhouse with his lawyer wife, Claire, loved jazz, fine wine, and designer sweaters; and never once wondered if status made him any less black. Though they were far from the ghetto, the Huxtables were unquestionably black and proud. This black family with class revolutionized America's image of black people and also revolutionized TV, showing that whites would watch a show filled with black characters in large numbers: From 1985 to 1990, *The Cosby Show* was #1 in the Nielsen ratings. Though some will still argue that the Huxtables's wealth and refinement made them unrealistic (as though there aren't any rich, cool black folks), the show was unflinchingly honest about the interactions among family members, from sibling rivalries to parental concern at children's choices. The Huxtables dressed well, but they also showed all the warts of the love/hate relationships that exist in real nuclear families. But that sort of artistic integrity has been a Cosby hallmark throughout his career. In four decades as a TV star, Cosby has brought a jazz attitude to bear, seeking not just to entertain, but to do so in a dignified way that takes full advantage of his prodigious intellect.

And from *Fat Albert* to *The Cosby Show*, he's sought to educate while he entertained and has focused on the dynamics and challenges of being in a family. That's why he's America's favorite Dad.

Bill Cosby, photographed by George Lange, 1985

Phylicia Rashad, circa 1988

Sarah Jessica Parker, photographed by Mary Ellen Mark, 1998

Goldie Hawn, 1968

goldie hawn **goldie hawn**

"I was a little nervous when I went on [*Rowan and Martin's Laugh In*]. And I'm a little bit dyslexic. Which means I'm not a lot dyslexic, but I do switch words sometimes and numbers sometimes. So the camera went on, and I got the words mixed up, and I started laughing. And I said to George, I said, 'George, I did it wrong.' And he said, 'That was just fine, Goldie,' Hence the character was created."

flip wilson ON ▶ **flip wilson**

"Most drag impersonations are a drag. But everyone can like Geraldine. The secret of my success with Geraldine is that she's not a put-down of women. She's smart, she's trustful, she's loyal, she's sassy. But women can like Geraldine, men can like Geraldine, everyone can like Geraldine."

Flip Wilson, 1972

The Moms, photographed by David LaChapelle, 1995. Clockwise from top left:
Florence Henderson (*The Brady Bunch*), Shirley Jones (*The Partridge Family*),
Marion Ross (*Happy Days*), June Lockhart (*Lassie*), Barbara Billingsley (*Leave
it to Beaver*), Jane Wyatt (*Father Knows Best*), and Esther Rolle (*Good Times*).

Richard Pryor, 1979

matthew perry  mary tyler moore

"I've been accused my entire professional career of stealing from Mr. Dick Van Dyke. That of course is not true. My entire career I've stolen from Mary Tyler Moore."

Mary Tyler Moore, 1970

Elizabeth Montgomery, 1967

Alfred Hitchcock, photographed by Phil Stern, circa 1948

alfred hitchcock **ON** > **alfred hitchcock**

"Television has brought murder back into the home—where it belongs."

peter falk ON ▷ peter falk

"Being chased by Columbo is like being nibbled to death by a duck."

 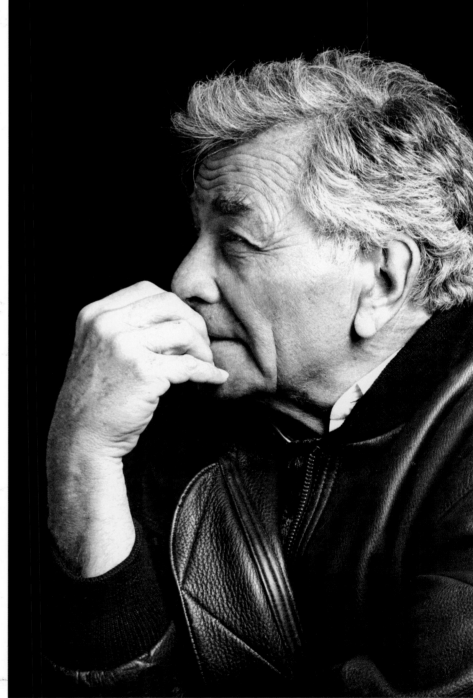

Peter Falk, photographed by Stephane Gizard, 2005

Ted Koppel, photographed by Theo Westenberger, 2000

Mike Wallace, photographed by Platon, 2003

James Garner, photographed by Annie Leibovitz, 1995

Michael Landon, 1954

Art Carney, circa 1950

art carney

"I love Ed Norton and what he did for my career. But the truth is that we couldn't have been more different. Norton was the total extrovert; there was no way you could put down his infectious good humor. Me? I'm a loner and a worrier."

Ray Romano, photographed by Sam Jones, 2003

Michael J. Fox, photographed by Mark Seliger, 1996

Jean Stapleton and Carroll O'Connor, photographed by Nigel Parry, 1995

Demond Wilson and Redd Foxx, as *Sanford and Son*'s Lamont and Fred G. Sanford, circa 1974

Bob Newhart, 1961

jon stewart **ON** ▷ bob newhart

"Before *The Bob Newhart Show*, there were only three things you could do in comedy: slip on something, run into something, or get poked. Newhart came along and said, I can be funny just sitting here with nothing happening."

george burns ON ▷ gracie allen

"Marrying Gracie was the best thing that ever happened to me. I have a feeling she felt the same way—that marrying her was the best thing that ever happened to me."

George Burns and Gracie Allen, 1954

the programs

The cast of
Cheers, 1982.
From top left:
Ted Danson,
Shelley Long,
Nicholas
Colasanto, and
Rhea Pearlman.

Tony Dow and Jerry Mathers of *Leave It to Beaver*, 1957

The cast of *The Brady Bunch*, 1970. Top row from left: Barry Williams, Florence Henderson, Eve Plumb, and Robert Reed. Bottom row from left: Christopher Knight, Susan Olsen, Maureen McCormick, and Mike Lookinland.

The cast of *Everybody Loves Raymond*, photographed by John P. Johnson, 2000.
Clockwise from top left: Doris Roberts, Brad Garrett, Peter Boyle, Patricia Heaton, and Ray Romano.

The cast of *Roots*, photographed by Herb Ritts, 1995. From left:
Ben Vereen, Leslie Uggams, John Amos, Cicely Tyson, and LeVar Burton

The cast of *Dallas*, photographed by Annie Leibovitz, 1995. From left: Larry Hagman, Victoria Principal, Charlene Tilton, Ken Kercheval, Steve Kanaly, Patrick Duffy, and Linda Gray.

**The cast of *Desperate Housewives*, photographed by Karin Catt, 2005. From left:
Nicolette Sheridan, Eva Longoria, Marcia Cross, Teri Hatcher, and Felicity Huffman.**

The cast of *Frasier*, photographed by Kate Garner, 1998. From left: Dan Butler, Peri Gilpin, Kelsey Grammer, David Hyde Pierce, Jane Leeves, and John Mahoney.

Edie Falco and James Gandolfini of *The Sopranos*, in a painting by Federico Castelluccio, photographed by Elizabeth Lippman, 2004

Cindy Williams and Penny Marshall of *Laverne and Shirley*, circa 1980

The cast of *Friends*, photographed by Annie Leibovitz, 2002. From left: David Schwimmer, Lisa Kudrow, Jennifer Aniston, Matthew Perry, Courtney Cox, and Matt LeBlanc.

The Westerners, photographed by Annie Leibovitz, 1995. From left, standing: Hugh O'Brian (*The Life and Legend of Wyatt Earp*), Clint Walker (*Cheyenne*), James Drury (*The Virginian*), Robert Horton (*Wagon Train*), Don Durant (*Johnny Ringo*), Peter Breck (*The Big Valley*), Lee Majors (*The Big Valley*), Robert Loggia (*The Nine Lives of Elfego Baca*), John Hart (*Hawkeye*), Sheb Wooley (*Rawhide*), Johnny Crawford (*The Rifleman*), Will Hutchins (*Sugarfoot*), David Carradine (*Kung Fu*), Ken Berry (*F Troop*), Larry Storch (*F Troop*), Michael Ansara (*Broken Arrow*), Clayton Moore (*The Lone Ranger*). From left, seated: Stuart Whitman (*Cimarron Strip*), Peter Brown (*The Lawman*), Gene Barry (*Bat Masterson*), Dale Robertson (*Tales of Wells Fargo*), Dick Simmons (*Sergeant Preston of the Yukon*), Fess Parker (*Daniel Boone, Davy Crockett*), Robert Culp (*Trackdown*), and Ben Murphy (*Alias Smith and Jones*).

KOMMANDANTUR

The cast of *Hogan's Heroes*, circa 1965. Clockwise from top left: Cynthia Lynn, Werner Klemperer, John Banner, Richard Dawson, Robert Clary, Ivan Dixon, and Bob Crane.

James Arness from *Gunsmoke*, 1967

Miss Piggy and Kermit the Frog of *The Muppet Show,* circa 1979

The cast of *The Munsters*, 1965. Clockwise from top left: Butch Patrick, Al Lewis, Fred Gwynne, and Yvonne DeCarlo.

mary tyler moore ON ▷ group therapy

TV comedy starts with great writing. That's a necessity. But I believe the next most important thing—the ingredient that will make a TV comedy endure—is a great ensemble cast.

There are no secret formulas to creating good television. The idea that launches a hit one season will produce an epidemic of copycat flops the next. Remember all those *Friends* clones that popped up after America fell in love with the Central Perk gang? Neither do I! Gathering together wonderful scripts, creating memorable characters, and finding the right cast is simply never easy. If you can do it right, you're going to run for a very long time. The characters created for us by the writers on *The Dick Van Dyke Show* and *Mary Tyler Moore*—well, we were each handed a great gift. There's no better way to say it—they were gifts.

In some ways, the ensemble cast is just the most visible evidence of the collaborative, group process behind all television. TV is never some genius sitting all alone writing whole scripts (well, except Carl Reiner!). More often the script is built up by many writers collaborating, feeding on each other's ideas. In fact, it was Carl Reiner who showed us all that you should take anybody's advice if it's good. If the man who makes the coffee has a good idea, put it in. You don't need credentials to have a good idea. On *The Dick Van Dyke Show* set, Carl always listened, whether to producers, the director, actors, and, yes, the guy who made the coffee.

The process of working within an ensemble is vital and energizing. The bigger the group, the more likely it is someone will have a good idea, a solution to some little problem, or a unique approach. The suggestions can come in from everywhere. The ensemble cast also give each character more relationships— and more possibilities. Think of how differently Mary Richards would relate to Lou or Rhoda or Phyllis. New facets of character come out of distinctive relationships. Another value of a large cast is that I believe it allows you to include characters who are larger-than-life, while still staying sufficiently grounded. Think of Ted Baxter or Georgette. You never knew what was going to come out of their mouths, and yet, within the larger group they remained believable.

And besides all that, having a large ensemble makes the whole experience more fun—these people truly become your family. You spend practically every waking hour with them. The more the merrier!

Of course, I have a personal affection for the ensembles I've been a part of— but there have been so many other wonderful ensemble casts over the years. From *M*A*S*H* to *Friends*, from *All in the Family* to *Taxi*. Think of how the *Cheers* cast changed over its run; a wonderful core ensemble also allows a show to evolve.

When it comes to what's on television today, I've become a fan of *The Office*. What a fascinating show and a wonderful example of a great ensemble. Of course, once again, it begins with the writing on that show, which is so absorbing, and funny.

Sometimes someone will say about this new show or that—"Oh look, they're doing what you guys did." But the resemblances are superficial. And after all there's room for more great ensemble work, more great characters, and more great TV.

The cast of *The Mary Tyler Moore Show*, 1970. From left: Cloris Leachman, Mary Tyler Moore, and Valerie Harper.

Patrick Macnee and Diana Rigg of *The Avengers*, 1965

Barbara Feldon and Don Adams of *Get Smart*, circa 1968

The cast of *Mission Impossible*, photographed by George Lange, 1995. From left: Peter Lupus, Greg Morris, Barbara Bain, Peter Graves, and Martin Landau.

The cast of *NYPD Blue*, photographed by Michael Grecco, 1994. From left: Nicholas Turturro, Dennis Franz, Jimmy Smits, Gordon Clapp, Sharon Lawrence, and James McDaniel.

The cast of *The Mod Squad*, photographed by David LaChapelle, 1995. From left: Clarence Williams III, Michael Cole, and Peggy Lipton.

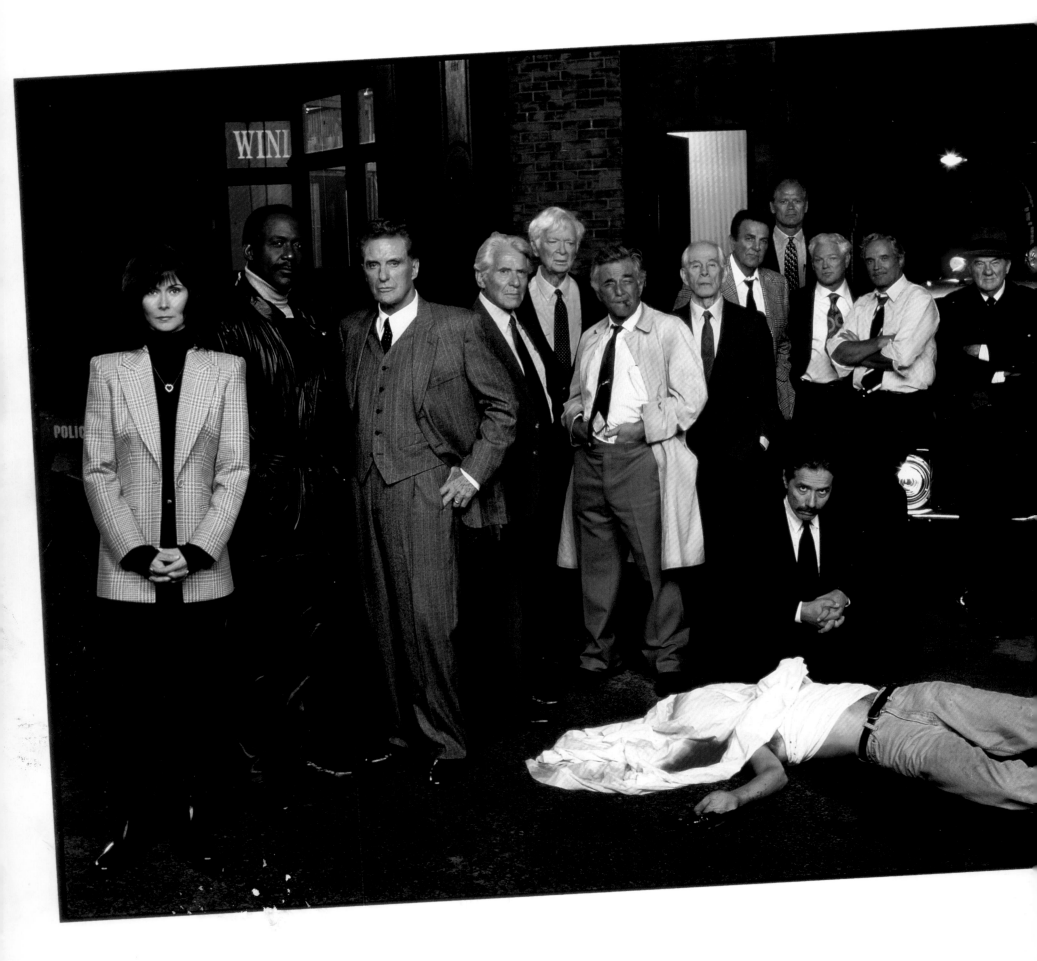

The Detectives, photographed by Annie Leibovitz, 1995. From left: Kate Jackson (*Charlie's Angels*), Richard Roundtree (*Shaft*), Robert Stack (*The Untouchables*), Efrem Zimbalist Jr. (*77 Sunset Strip, The F.B.I.*), Buddy Ebsen (*Barnaby Jones*), Peter Falk (*Columbo*), Harry Morgan (*Dragnet*), Edward James Olmos (*Miami Vice*), who is kneeling, Mike Connors (*Mannix*), Fred Dryer (*Hunter*), James MacArthur (*Hawaii Five-O*), Hal Linden (*Barney Miller*), Karl Malden (*The Streets of San Francisco*), Anthony Eisley (*Hawaiian Eye*), Sharon Gless and Tyne Daly (*Cagney & Lacey*), Jimmy Smits and Dennis Franz (*NYPD Blue*), Angie Dickinson (*Police Woman*), Don Johnson (*Miami Vice*), Craig Stevens (*Peter Gunn*), Angela Lansbury (*Murder, She Wrote*), and Robert Wagner (*Hart to Hart*).

The cast of *Saturday Night Live*, photographed by Edie Baskin, circa 1978. From left: Garrett Morris, Jane Curtin, Bill Murray, Laraine Newman, Dan Aykroyd, Gilda Ratner, and John Belushi.

The cast of *In Living Color*, photographed by Andrew Semel, 1990. Top row, from left: Marc Wilmore, Jim Carrey, Anne-Marie Johnson, and Jay Leggett. Middle row, from left: T'Keyah Keymah, Jamie Foxx, and Carol Rosenthal. Bottom row, from left: Tommy Davidson, Alexandra Wentworth, and David Alan Grier.

The cast of *Monty Python's Flying Circus*, 1971.
From left: Eric Idle, Graham Chapman, Michael
Palin, John Cleese, Terry Jones, and Terry Gilliam.

The cast of *Rowan and Martin's Laugh In*, photographed by David LaChapelle, 1995. Top row, from left: Gary Owens, Alan Sues, and Dave Madden (in windows); Ruth Buzzi, Dick Martin, Chelsea Brown (on cake). Bottom, from left: Jo Anne Worley and Henry Gibson.

credits

bill cosby
Eddie Adams/Corbis Outline

carol burnett
Greg Watermann/Corbis Outline

danny devito
George Lange/Corbis Outline

milton berle
NBC/Globe Photos, Inc.

oprah winfrey
Cliff Watts/Harpo Productions, Inc.

jackie gleason
Philippe Halsman/Magnum Photos

jack webb
Thurston Hopkins/Hulton Archive/Getty Images

sid caesar and imogene coca
Firooz Zahedi/JBGPhoto.com

lucille ball
Globe Photos, Inc.

ellen degeneres
Nigel Parry/CPi

will smith
Annie Leibovitz/Contact Press Images

larry david
Jill Greenberg/Corbis Outline

jimmie walker
Globe Photos, Inc.

freddie prinze
NBC/Globe Photos, Inc.

jay leno
Annie Leibovitz/Contact Press Images

jack paar
Nigel Parry/CPi

ed asner
MTM Enterprises/The Kobal Collection

tom brokaw, dan rather, and peter jennings
Annie Leibovitz/Contact Press Images

dick van dyke and mary tyler moore
Annie Leibovitz/Contact Press Images

carol burnett
Jack Chuck/Corbis Outline

conan o'brien
Gavin Bond/Corbis Outline

larry king
Michael O'Neill for Vanity Fair/Corbis Outline

dick clark
Paul Schutzer/Time & Life Pictures/Getty Images

edward r. murrow
Hulton Archive/Getty Images

johnny carson
CBS Photo Archive/Hulton Archive/Getty Images

howard cosell
Focus On Sport/Getty Images

phil donahue
Globe Photos, Inc.

alan alda
Gene Trindl/Globe Photos, Inc.

raymond burr
Yousuf Karsh/Camera Press/Retna Ltd.

bea arthur
CBS Photo Archive/Hulton Archive/Getty Images

walter cronkite
Michael O'Neill for Vanity Fair/Corbis Outline

katie couric
Jonathan Skow/Corbis Outline

barbara walters
Yousuf Karsh/Camera Press/Retna Ltd.

andy rooney
Platon/CPi

regis philbin
Danny Clinch/Corbis Outline

bob denver
CBS Photo Archive/Getty Images

sally field
Screen Gems/The Kobal Collection

candice bergen
Mary Ellen Mark

fred rogers
Photofest/Retna Ltd.

jim henson
Rex USA

robin williams
Firooz Zahedi/JBGPhoto.com

carl reiner
Hulton Archive/Getty Images

bob hope
Annie Leibovitz/Contact Press Images

eddie murphy
Timothy White/Corbis Outline

roseanne barr
Peggy Sirota/Corbis Outline

barbara eden and larry hagman
NBC/Globe Photos, Inc.

jack benny and marilyn monroe
Keystone/Hulton Archive/Getty Images

ed sullivan
Allan Grant/Time & Life Pictures/Getty Images

diahann carroll
Hulton Archive/Getty Images

henry winkler
John R. Hamilton/Globe Photos, Inc.

david janssen
Gene Trindl/Globe Photos, Inc.

rod serling
Hulton Archive/Getty Images

leonard nimoy
Lillian Elaine Wilson/Contour Photos

william shatner
Jeffery Newbury/Corbis Outline

ron howard
Xavier Torres-Bacchetta/Corbis Outline

don knotts and andy griffith
Hulton Archive/Getty Images

joan collins
The Kobal Collection

farrah fawcett
Henry Groskinsky/Time & Life Pictures/Getty Images

bill cosby
George Lange/Corbis Outline

phylicia rashad
NBC-TV /The Kobal Collection

sarah jessica parker
Mary Ellen Mark

goldie hawn
Hulton Archive/Getty Images

flip wilson
NBC/Globe Photos, Inc.

the moms
David LaChapelle/Contour Photos

richard pryor
C City/Globe Photos, Inc.

mary tyler moore
Photofest/Retna Ltd.

elizabeth montgomery
Rex USA

alfred hitchcock
Phil Stern/CPi

peter falk
Stephane Gizard/Starface/Retna Ltd.

ted koppel
Theo Westenberger/Corbis Outline

mike wallace
Platon/CPi

james garner
Annie Leibovitz/Contact Press Images

michael landon
Hulton Archive/Getty Images

art carney
CBS/Landov

ray romano
Sam Jones/Corbis Outline

michael j. fox
Mark Seliger/Corbis Outline

jean stapleton and carroll o'connor
Nigel Parry/CPi

demond wilson and redd foxx
NBC/Globe Photos, Inc.

bob newhart
The Kobal Collection

george burns and gracie allen
CBS Photo Archive/Hulton Archive/Getty Images

cheers
The Kobal Collection

leave it to beaver
Hulton Archive/Getty Images

the brady bunch
Photofest/Retna Ltd.

everybody loves raymond
John P. Johnson/Corbis Outline

roots
Herb Ritts/Lime Foto

dallas
Annie Leibovitz/Contact Press Images

desperate housewives
Karin Catt /Lime Foto

frasier
Kate Garner/Corbis Outline

the sopranos
Elizabeth Lippman/Contour Photos

laverne and shirley
Paramount Television/The Kobal Collection

friends
Annie Leibovitz/Contact Press Images

the westerners
Annie Leibovitz/Contact Press Images

hogan's heroes
CBS Photo Archive/Hulton Archive/Getty Images

gunsmoke
CBS Photo Archive/Hulton Archive/Getty Images

the muppet show
ATV/Henson Associates/The Kobal Collection

the odd couple
Hulton Archive/Getty Images

will and grace
Robert Trachtenberg/Corbis Outline

the sonny and cher show
The Kobal Collection

the jeffersons
CBS-TV/The Kobal Collection

the addams family
ABC-TV/The Kobal Collection

the munsters
CBS Photo Archive/Getty Images

the mary tyler moore show
CBS-TV /The Kobal Collection

the avengers
The Kobal Collection

get smart
CBS-TV/NBC/Talent Assoc/The Kobal Collection

mission impossible
George Lange/Corbis Outline

nypd blue
Michael Grecco/Icon International

the mod squad
David LaChapelle/Contour Photos

the tv cops/detectives
Annie Leibovitz/Contact Press Images

saturday night live
Edie Baskin/Corbis Outline

in living color
Fox-TV/The Kobal Collection

monty python's flying circus
Columbia/The Kobal Collection

rowan & martin's laugh-in
David LaChapelle/Contour Photos

the icons

ALAN ALDA starred in *M*A*S*H* from 1972 to 1983.

GRACIE ALLEN starred in *The George Burns and Gracie Allen Show* from 1950 to 1958.

BEA ARTHUR starred in *Maude* from 1972 to 1978 and in *The Golden Girls* from 1985 to 1992.

ED ASNER starred in *The Mary Tyler Moore Show* from 1970 to 1977 and in *Lou Grant* from 1977 to 1982.

LUCILLE BALL starred in *I Love Lucy* from 1951 to 1957.

ROSEANNE BARR starred in *Roseanne* from 1988 to 1997.

JACK BENNY starred in *The Jack Benny Program* from 1950 to 1965.

CANDICE BERGEN starred in *Murphy Brown* from 1988 to 1998.

MILTON BERLE starred in *The Milton Berle Show* from 1948 to 1956.

BARBARA BILLINGSLEY starred in *Leave it to Beaver* from 1957 to 1963.

TOM BROKAW anchored the *NBC Nightly News* from 1982 to 2004.

CAROL BURNETT starred in *The Carol Burnett Show* from 1967 to 1978.

GEORGE BURNS starred in *The George Burns and Gracie Allen Show* from 1950 to 1958.

RAYMOND BURR starred in *Perry Mason* from 1957 to 1966 and in *Ironside* from 1967 to 1975.

SID CAESAR and **IMOGENE COCA** starred in *Your Show of Shows* from 1950 to 1954.

ART CARNEY starred in *The Honeymooners* from 1955 to 1956.

DIAHANN CARROLL starred in *Julia* from 1968 to 1971.

JOHNNY CARSON hosted *The Tonight Show* from 1962 to 1992.

DICK CLARK hosted *American Bandstand* from 1952 to 1989.

JOAN COLLINS starred in *Dynasty* from 1981 to 1989.

BILL COSBY starred in *The Cosby Show* from 1984 to 1992.

HOWARD COSELL hosted *NFL Monday Night Football* from 1970 to 1983.

KATIE COURIC hosted *The Today Show* from 1991 to 2006.

WALTER CRONKITE anchored the *CBS Evening News* from 1962 to 1981.

LARRY DAVID co-created *Seinfeld* in 1990 and served as executive producer until 1996. He created and has starred in *Curb Your Enthusiasm* since 1999.

ELLEN DEGENERES starred in *Ellen* from 1994 to 1998 and has hosted *The Ellen DeGeneres Show* since 2003.

BOB DENVER starred in *The Many Lives of Dobie Gillis* from 1959 to 1963 and *Gilligan's Island* from 1964 to 1967.

DANNY DEVITO starred in *Taxi* from 1978 to 1983.

PHIL DONAHUE hosted *The Phil Donahue Show* from 1970 to 1996.

DICK VAN DYKE starred in *The Dick Van Dyke Show* from 1961 to 1966.

BARBARA EDEN starred in *I Dream of Jeannie* from 1965 to 1970.

PETER FALK starred as *Columbo* from 1971 to 1978 and from 1989 to 2003.

FARRAH FAWCETT starred in *Charlie's Angels* from 1976 to 1977.

SALLY FIELD starred in *Gidget* from 1965 to 1966 and in *The Flying Nun* from 1967 to 1970.

MICHAEL J. FOX starred in *Family Ties* from 1982 to 1989 and in *Spin City* from 1996 to 2000.

REDD FOXX starred in *Sanford and Son* from 1972 to 1977.

JAMES GARNER starred in *The Rockford Files* from 1974 to 1980.

JACKIE GLEASON starred in *The Honeymooners* from 1955 to 1956.

ANDY GRIFFITH starred in *The Andy Griffith Show* from 1960 to 1968 and in *Matlock* from 1986 to 1995.

LARRY HAGMAN starred in *I Dream of Jeannie* from 1965 to 1970 and in *Dallas* from 1978 to 1991.

GOLDIE HAWN starred in *Rowan and Martin's Laugh-In* from 1968 to 1970.

FLORENCE HENDERSON starred in *The Brady Bunch* from 1969 to 1974.

JIM HENSON created and starred in *The Muppet Show* from 1976 to 1981 and *Sesame Street* from 1969 to 1990.

ALFRED HITCHCOCK hosted *Alfred Hitchcock Presents* from 1955 to 1962.

BOB HOPE hosted *Bob Hope Presents the Chrysler Theatre* from 1963 to 1967 and a series of specials and variety shows until the early '90s."

RON HOWARD starred in *The Andy Griffith Show* from 1960 to 1968 and in *Happy Days* from 1974 to 1980.

DAVID JANSSEN starred in *The Fugitive* from 1963 to 1967.

PETER JENNINGS anchored *ABC World News Tonight* from 1983 to 2005.

SHIRLEY JONES starred in *The Partridge Family* from 1970 to 1974.

LARRY KING has hosted *Larry King Live* since 1985.

DON KNOTTS starred in *The Andy Griffith Show* from 1960 to 1968 and in *Three's Company* from 1979 to 1984.

TED KOPPEL anchored *ABC News Nightline* from 1981 to 2005.

MICHAEL LANDON starred in *Bonanza* from 1965 to 1973, *Little House on the Prairie* from 1974 to 1983, and in *Highway to Heaven* from 1984 to 1989.

JAY LENO has hosted *The Tonight Show* since 1992.

JUNE LOCKHART starred in *Lassie* from 1958 to 1964 and in *Lost in Space* from 1965 to 1968.

ELIZABETH MONTGOMERY starred in *Bewitched* from 1964 to 1972.

MARY TYLER MOORE starred in *The Dick Van Dyke Show* from 1961 to 1966 and in *The Mary Tyler Moore Show* from 1970 to 1977.

EDDIE MURPHY starred in *Saturday Night Live* from 1980 to 1984.

EDWARD R. MURROW hosted *See it Now* from 1951 to 1958.

BOB NEWHART starred in *The Bob Newhart Show* from 1972 to 1978 and in *Newhart* from 1982 to 1990.

LEONARD NIMOY starred in *Star Trek* from 1966 to 1969.

CONAN O'BRIEN has hosted *Late Night with Conan O'Brien* since 1993.

CARROLL O'CONNOR starred in *All in the Family* from 1971 to 1979.

JACK PAAR hosted *The Jack Paar Tonight Show* from 1957 to 1962.

SARAH JESSICA PARKER starred in *Sex and the City* from 1998 to 2004.

REGIS PHILBIN has co-hosted *Live with Regis and Kathie Lee/Live with Regis and Kelly* since 1989.

FREDDIE PRINZE starred in *Chico and the Man* from 1974 to 1978.

RICHARD PRYOR starred in *The Richard Pryor Show* in 1977.

PHYLICIA RASHAD starred in *The Cosby Show* from 1984 to 1992.

DAN RATHER anchored *The CBS Evening News* from 1981 to 2005.

CARL REINER starred in *Your Show of Shows* from 1950 to 1954. He created *The Dick Van Dyke Show* in 1961, which ran until 1966.

FRED ROGERS starred in *Mister Rogers' Neighborhood* from 1968 to 2001.

ESTHER ROLLE starred in *Good Times* from 1974 to 1979.

RAY ROMANO starred in *Everybody Loves Raymond* from 1996 to 2005.

ANDY ROONEY has served as a commentator for *60 Minutes* since 1978.

MARION ROSS starred in *Happy Days* from 1974 to 1984.

ROD SERLING created and hosted *The Twilight Zone* from 1959 to 1964.

WILLIAM SHATNER starred in *Star Trek* from 1966 to 1969.

WILL SMITH starred in *The Fresh Prince of Bel-Air* from 1990 to 1996.

JEAN STAPLETON starred in *All in the Family* from 1971 to 1979.

ED SULLIVAN hosted *The Ed Sullivan Show* from 1948 to 1971.

JIMMIE WALKER starred in *Good Times* from 1974 to 1979.

MIKE WALLACE has co-hosted *60 Minutes* since 1968.

BARBARA WALTERS co-anchored *20/20* from 1984 to 2004 and has co-hosted *The View* since 1997.

JACK WEBB starred in *Dragnet* from 1951 to 1959.

ROBIN WILLIAMS starred in *Mork and Mindy* from 1978 to 1982.

DEMOND WILSON starred in *Sanford and Son* from 1972 to 1977.

FLIP WILSON starred in *The Flip Wilson Show* from 1970 to 1974.

OPRAH WINFREY has hosted *The Oprah Winfrey Show* since 1986.

HENRY WINKLER starred in *Happy Days* from 1974 to 1984.

JANE WYATT starred in *Father Knows Best* from 1954 to 1960.

the programs

77 Sunset Strip ran on ABC from 1958 to 1964.

Alias Smith and Jones ran on ABC from 1971 to 1973.

Barnaby Jones ran on CBS from 1973 to 1980.

Barney Miller ran on ABC from 1975 to 1982.

Bat Masterson ran on NBC from 1958 to 1961.

Broken Arrow ran on ABC from 1956 to 1960.

Cagney & Lacey ran on CBS from 1982 to 1988.

Charlie's Angels ran on ABC from 1976 to 1981.

Cheers ran on NBC from 1982 to 1993.

Cheyenne ran on ABC from 1955 to 1963.

Cimarron Strip ran on CBS from 1967 to 1968.

Columbo ran in syndication from 1971 to 1978 and 1989 to 2003.

Dallas ran on CBS from 1978 to 1991.

Daniel Boone ran on NBC from 1964 to 1970.

Davy Crockett ran on ABC in 1954.

Desperate Housewives debuted on ABC in 2005.

Dragnet ran on NBC from 1951 to 1959.

Everybody Loves Raymond ran on CBS from 1996 to 2005.

F Troop ran on ABC from 1965 to 1967.

Frasier ran on NBC from 1993 to 2004.

Friends ran on NBC from 1994 to 2004.

Get Smart ran on CBS from 1965 to 1970.

Gunsmoke ran on CBS from 1955 to 1975.

Hart to Hart ran on ABC from 1979 to 1984.

Hawaii Five-O ran on CBS from 1968 to 1980.

Hawaiian Eye ran on ABC from 1959 to 1963.

Hawkeye ran in syndication in 1957.

Hogan's Heroes ran on CBS from 1965 to 1971.

Hunter ran on NBC from 1984 to 1991.

In Living Color ran on FOX from 1990 to 1994.

Johnny Ringo ran on CBS from 1959 to 1960.

Kung Fu ran on ABC from 1972 to 1975.

Laverne and Shirley ran on ABC from 1976 to 1983.

Leave it to Beaver ran on CBS from 1957 to 1963.

Mannix ran on CBS from 1967 to 1975.

Miami Vice ran on ABC from 1984 to 1989.

Mission: Impossible ran on CBS from 1966 to 1973.

Monty Python's Flying Circus ran on BBC from 1969 to 1974.

Murder, She Wrote ran on CBS from 1984 to 1996.

NYPD Blue ran on ABC from 1993 to 2005.

Peter Gunn ran on NBC from 1958 to 1960 and ABC from 1960 to 1961.

Police Woman ran on NBC from 1974 to 1978.

Rawhide ran on CBS from 1959 to 1966.

Roots ran on ABC in 1977.

Rowan & Martin's Laugh-In ran on NBC from 1968 to 1973.

Saturday Night Live debuted on NBC in 1975.

Sergeant Preston of the Yukon ran on CBS from 1955 to 1958.

Shaft ran on CBS from 1973 to 1974.

Sugarfoot ran on ABC from 1957 to 1961.

Tales of Wells Fargo ran on NBC from 1957 to 1962.

The Addams Family ran on ABC from 1964 to 1966.

The Avengers ran on ABC from 1961 to 1969.

The Big Valley ran on ABC from 1965 to 1969.

The Brady Bunch ran on ABC from 1969 to 1974.

The F.B.I. ran on ABC from 1965 to 1974.

The Jeffersons ran on CBS from 1975 to 1985.

The Lawman ran on ABC from 1958 to 1962.

The Life and Legend of Wyatt Earp ran on ABC from 1955 to 1961.

The Lone Ranger ran on ABC from 1949 to 1957.

The Mary Tyler Moore Show ran on CBS from 1970 to 1977.

The Mod Squad ran on ABC from 1968 to 1973.

The Munsters ran on CBS from 1964 to 1966.

The Muppet Show ran on CBS from 1976 to 1981.

The Nine Lives of Elfego Baca ran on ABC in 1958.

The Odd Couple ran on ABC from 1970 to 1975.

The Rifleman ran on ABC from 1958 to 1963.

The Sonny and Cher Show ran on CBS from 1976 to 1977.

The Sopranos debuted on HBO in 1999.

The Streets of San Francisco ran on ABC from 1972 to 1977.

The Untouchables ran on ABC from 1959 to 1963.

The Virginian ran on NBC from 1962 to 1971.

Trackdown ran on CBS from 1957 to 1959.

Wagon Train ran on NBC from 1957 to 1962 and ABC from 1962 to 1965.

Will and Grace ran on NBC from 1998 to 2006.

acknowledgments

A huge thanks to those who helped make
TV Land Legends worthy of those it honors:

David E. Brown, Louise Burke, Karen Cummins,
Juline Douglas, Jeff Dymowski, Jennifer Heddle,
Tom Hill, Larry Jones, Kenna Kay, Joe Manghise,
Margaret Milnes, Lauren Moosbrugger, Lauren
Nathan, Rob Pellizzi, David Rieth, Lia Ronnen,
Michael Rowe, Chris Sabin, John Sanchez, Caroline
Schneider, Jeffrey D. Smith, Lindsey Stanberry,
Betty Wong, Megan Worman, Anthony Ziccardi,
and all the photographers who beautifully captured
the legends that keep us inspired.

This book was produced by Melcher Media, Inc.
124 West 13th Street
New York, NY 10011
www.melcher.com

Publisher: Charles Melcher
Associate Publisher: Bonnie Eldon
Editor in Chief: Duncan Bock
Editor: Holly Rothman
Assistant Editor: Shoshana Thaler
Production Director: Andrea Hirsh

Design by Helene Silverman
Photography Editing by Nadine Raia Desiderio
Text Research by Patrick Carone

Front Cover: Don Knotts and Andy Griffith
Hulton archive/Getty Images, 1965
Back Cover: Lucille Ball and Desi Arnaz
Globe Photos Inc., circa 1955